.

Women's Leadership Quotes

Inspiring Quotes from Female Leaders

First Research Paradigms Applied Edition, March 2022

What Can MBA Do in My Workday?
Edited book collection

Alex Stajković, *Editor in Chief*
Kayla Sergent, *Executive Editor*

This edited collection aims to advance evidence-based application of the topics typically covered in the MBA programs.

Book 1. Management and Leadership
  by Alex Stajković and Kayla Sergent

Book 2. Women's Leadership Quotes
  by Kayla and Alex Stajković

LIBRARY OF CONGRESS CONTROL NUMBER: 2022933970

ISBN: 978-1-7338275-1-5

About the Authors

Alex Stajković, Ph.D.
Professor of Organizational Behavior
M. Keith Weikel Distinguished Chair
in Leadership
Wisconsin School of Business
University of Wisconsin-Madison.
www.stajkovic.biz

Kayla Stajkovic, Ph.D., CPA
Assistant Professor of
Organizational Behavior
Edgewood College
www.kstajkovic.com

Dedication

To our inspirational mothers:
Zorica Stajkovic and *Monica Sergent*

Introduction

Leadership knowledge creation in industrial and organizational psychology is routinely directed toward business agendas. There is nothing wrong with that. Society needs successfuly-led private enterprises that benefit many people.

However, recent research on women's leadership shows that many people are left out of private enterprise economic prosperity. For example, as the economic health of cities in the United States increases so, too, does racial inequality. Some of the wealthiest urban areas have the most homelessness. The Black Lives Matter movement exposed many inequality gaps, and COVID-19 compounded these gaps with its disproportionate impact on minority communities.

Leadership research in applied psychology is often aimed at improving leadership effectiveness, but little of it invigorates efforts at public engagement in solving 21st century societal problems. Leadership literature needs to expand from mostly an academic study of the mind and abstract behaviors to an exercise in actionable knowledge creation and application to social welfare.

Public leadership is about relationships between the science of leadership and society. Purveyors of change need to build bridges between leadership scholars and consumers of leadership knowledge in the public.

There is no an easy roadmap toward social transformation through public leadership. Solving social problems requires collaborative partnerships, participatory involvement, and public engagement.

Counter to prevailing notions of *think-manager, think-male* in which a preferred leadership style was thought to be one more often associated with masculinity - autocratic, decisive, and controlling, recent research shows that in a social crisis, women seem to be more effective leaders. For example, in our Journal of Applied Psychology article, we found that states with a woman governor were associated with fewer COVID-19 deaths during early stages of the global pandemic compared to states with a male governor. A text analysis of governors' briefings revealed that women governors displayed greater empathy and confidence in their speeches. These strong women leaders spoke about issues relevant to their followers, and they embodied compassion for how their people might be feeling during unprecendended times. Women governors also conveyed more confidence in a brighter future ahead. Studies continue to emerge supporting a female leadership advantage in a crisis.

This book is dedicated to this emerging research stream. It provides practical qualitative illustrations of effective women leaders throughout history.

Public leadership is an urgent and unfinished project. By summarizing and presenting quotes in one place, this book represents a modest attempt to contribute meaningfully toward building an architecture of leadership through the lenses of women leaders.

Jacinda Ardern
40th Prime Minister of New Zealand

"One of the criticisms I've faced over the years is that I'm not aggressive enough or assertive enough or maybe somehow, because I'm empathetic, it means I'm weak. I totally rebel against that. I refuse to believe that you cannot be both compassionate and strong."

"Rarely are opportunities presented to you in a perfect way - in a nice little box with a yellow bow on top. 'Here, open it, it's perfect. You'll love it.' Opportunities – the good ones – are messy, confusing and hard to recognize. They're risky. They challenge you."

Susan Wojcicki
CEO of YouTube

Eleanor Roosevelt
First Lady of the United States, 1933-1945

"A mature person is one who does not think only in absolutes, who is able to be objective even when deeply stirred emotionally, who has learned that there is both good and bad in all people and in all things, and who walks humbly and deals charitably with the circumstances of life, knowing that in this world no one is all knowing and, therefore, all of us need both love and charity."

"Do the one thing you think you cannot do. Fail at it. Try again. Do better the second time. The only people who never tumble are those who never mount the wire. This is your moment. Own it."

Oprah Winfrey
Media Executive and Philanthropist

Indra Nooyi
CEO of PepsiCo, 2006-2018

"Leadership is hard to define, and good leadership even harder. But if you can get people to follow you to the ends of the earth, you are a great leader."

"Take criticism seriously, but not personally. If there is truth or merit in the criticism, try to learn from it. Otherwise, let it roll right off you."

Hillary Clinton
First Lady of the United States, 1993-2001
67th United States Secretary of State

Sheryl Sandberg
COO of Facebook

"Leadership is about making others better as a result of your presence and making sure that impact lasts in your absence."

"We must believe that we are gifted for something, and that this thing, at whatever cost, must be attained."

Marie Curie
Nobel Prize in Physics, 1903
Nobel Prize in Chemistry, 1911

Kristi Noem
33rd Governor of South Dakota

"A lot of people have tried to put labels on me, but right now I'm focused on being Kristi Noem and getting my message out to South Dakotans."

"Define success on your own terms, achieve it by your own rules, and build a life you're proud to live."

Anne Sweeney
President of Disney ABC Television Group, 1996-2014

Margaret Mead
American Anthropologist

"Never doubt that a small group of thoughtful committed citizens can change the world. Indeed, it is the only thing that ever has."

"Dreams do not come true just because you dream them. It's hard work that makes things happen. It's hard work that creates change."

Shonda Rhimes
American Writer and Film Producer

Rosa Parks
American Civil Rights Activist

"I have learned over the years that when one's mind is made up, this diminishes fear; knowing what must be done does away with fear."

"It's okay to admit what you don't know. It's okay to ask for help. And it's more than okay to listen to the people you lead – in fact, it's essential."

Mary Barra
CEO of General Motors

Ayn Rand
American Writer and Philosopher

"The question isn't who is going to let me; it's who is going to stop me?"

"I have a relatively sunny spirit, and I always had the expectation that my path through life would be relatively sunny, no matter what happened. I have never allowed myself to be bitter."

Angela Merkel
34th Chancellor of Germany

Anna Wintour
Editor-in-Chief of Vogue

"People respond well to those that are sure of what they want."

"A leader takes people where they want to go. A great leader takes people where they don't necessarily want to go but ought to be."

Rosalynn Carter
First Lady of the United States, 1977-1981

Diana
Princess of Wales, 1981 - 1997

"I don't go by the rule book. I lead from the heart, not the head."

"We treat our people like royalty. If you honor and serve the people who work for you, they will honor and serve you."

Mary Kay Ash
Founder of Mary Kay Cosmetics

Ellen Johnson Sirleaf
24th President of Liberia

"The size of your dreams must always exceed your current capacity to achieve them. If your dreams do not scare you, they are not big enough."

"No matter what your current ability is, effort is what ignites that ability and turns it into accomplishment."

Carol Dweck
American Psychologist

Abigail Johnson
President and CEO of Fidelity Investments

"No matter how senior you get in an organization, no matter how well you're perceived to be doing, your job is never done."

"How does a queen bee behave? However she wants to. But please don't wait for someone to hold the door open for you when your own arms work perfectly fine - do it yourself."

Whitney Wolfe Herd
CEO of Bumble, Inc.

Queen Elizabeth II

"I know of no single formula for success. But over the years, I have observed that some attributes of leadership are universal and are often about finding ways of encouraging people to combine their efforts, their talents, their insights, their enthusiasm, and their inspiration to work together."

"It was we, the people, not we, the white male citizens, nor yet we, the male citizens; but we, the whole people, who formed this Union. And we formed it, not to give the blessings or liberty, but to secure them; not to the half of ourselves and the half of our posterity, but to the whole people - women as well as men."

Susan B. Anthony
American Social Reformer and Activist

Gretchen Whitmer
49th Governor of Michigan

"In an era when so many women are stepping up to lead, I'm hoping people will focus on our ideas and accomplishments instead of our appearance."

"The fastest way to break the cycle of perfectionism and become a fearless mother is to give up the idea of doing it perfectly - indeed to embrace unertainty and imperfection."

Arianna Huffington
Founder of the Huffington Post

Christine Lagarde
President of the European Central Bank

"I have a theory that women are generally given space and appointed to jobs when the situation is tough. I've observed that in many instances. In times of crisis, women eventually are called upon to sort out the mess, face the difficult issues, and be completely focused on restoring the situation."

"Strong men - men who are truly role models - don't need to put down women to make themselves feel powerful. People who are truly strong lift others up. People who are truly powerful bring others together."

Michelle Obama
First Lady of the United States, 2009-2017

Saint Therese of Lisieux

"Without love, deeds, even the most brilliant, count as nothing."

Index

Jacinda Ardern 2-3

Susan Wojcicki 4-5

Eleanor Roosevelt 6-7

Oprah Winfrey 8-9

Indra Nooyi 10-11

Hillary Clinton 12-13

Sheryl Sandberg 14-15

Marie Curie 16-17

Kristi Noem 18-19

Anne Sweeney 20-21

Margaret Mead 22-23

Shonda Rhimes 24-25

Rosa Parks 26-27

Mary Barra 28-29

Ayn Rand 30-31

Angela Merkel 32-33

Anna Wintour 34-35

Rosalynn Carter 36-37

Princess Diana 38-39

Mary Kay Ash 40-41

Ellen Johnson Sirleaf 42-43

Carol Dweck 44-45

Abigail Johnson 46-47

Whitney Wolfe Herd 48-49

Queen Elizabeth II 50-51

Susan B. Anthony 52-53

Gretchen Whitmer 54-55

Arianna Huffington 56-57

Christine Lagarde 58-59

Michelle Obama 60-61

Saint Therese of Lisieux 62-63